T0123510

REFLECTIONS

MOMENTS IN TIME

Joyce Henefield Coleman

REFLECTIONS
MOMENTS IN TIME

Copyright © 2021 Joyce Henefield Coleman.

All rights reserved. No part of this book may be used or reproduced by any means, graphic, electronic, or mechanical, including photocopying, recording, taping or by any information storage retrieval system without the written permission of the author except in the case of brief quotations embodied in critical articles and reviews.

iUniverse books may be ordered through booksellers or by contacting:

iUniverse
1663 Liberty Drive
Bloomington, IN 47403
www.iuniverse.com
844-349-9409

Because of the dynamic nature of the Internet, any web addresses or links contained in this book may have changed since publication and may no longer be valid. The views expressed in this work are solely those of the author and do not necessarily reflect the views of the publisher, and the publisher hereby disclaims any responsibility for them.

Any people depicted in stock imagery provided by Getty Images are models, and such images are being used for illustrative purposes only.
Certain stock imagery © Getty Images.

ISBN: 978-1-6632-3045-4 (sc)
ISBN: 978-1-6632-3047-8 (hc)
ISBN: 978-1-6632-3046-1 (e)

Library of Congress Control Number: 2021923730

Print information available on the last page.

iUniverse rev. date: 11/24/2021

Jack, this book is for you. You led a remarkable life both through good times and bad. I feel honored to have shared it with you. Thank you for including so many people into our family. Each has brought us much joy and happiness. You are missed but remain in our hearts.

As in most projects, a team of people are needed to complete the task. Publishing "Reflections" has involved a team of people. I personally wish to thank and acknowledge their talents and expertise. The design on the book cover was created by Junnifer Baya. Courtney Wallace and Mitchel Monahan coordinated the editing process and kept me on task. My daughter Jacque Havelka assisted me throughout the entire process. Alfred Riley is assisting in the Marketing of this book. A heartfelt thanks to all. It truly takes a village to publish a book.

"But how could you live and have no story to tell?
Fyodor Dostoyevsky"

CONTENTS

PREFACE

Reflecting upon one's past can be joyous but also sad. As humans, we are prone to dwell upon the sad and disappointing events rather than those that were happy. However, we often learn more about ourselves when we experience the disappointing and sad times. Sometimes we have to dig deep down in our inner being to find that spark of insight, that truth about ourselves that helps us to grow as human beings. There have been some very sad times and difficult losses in my life that I struggled to get through, but, in the end, they gave me strength that I did not know I had. They taught me the value of loss and sadness and to look to the light and the joy that was around me. I have learned to look for joy and excitement in the little things around me. I have also learned to look for the beauty in reading and writing. We take everything around us for granted because we are so busy in our lives. I remember those busy days when I fell into bed exhausted from all that I had done during the day. I learned from those many years of juggling the things in my life the importance of taking time to look around me for the beauty that is there and to appreciate the little things in life. I am amazed at all the beauty I have observed around me that for years I ignored or simply wasn't aware of. Our lives will continue to be full of activities and disruptions, but it is important to also stop and look around for the beauty, the joy, and the simple things in life. They enrich our lives.

Write down your life stories. It is important to record and to share them. Our lives are composed of many stories just waiting to be told. They are important to those to come. I have many questions about my ancestors that I wish I could ask. There are many "why's" I would like answered. Hopefully, my poetry and writings will give my ancestors to come an insight into who I was, and perhaps, even answer some of their "why's".

REFLECTIONS

I stand on the mount of time
Looking back across the years
More years than I dreamed possible
A melding of joys, beauty, loss and pain
What seemed like a puzzle now is clearer
The Master plan unfolds ever so slowly
So many hills and valleys to traverse
Burdens that must be carried
Inexplicable joys to experience and celebrate
Not all of the "whys" are answered
But life does have a purpose
One is blessed to have a glimpse of it
To feel that life has been worthwhile
That one has fulfilled their purpose

THIS MORNING

This morning the air is crisp
Night coolness is slowly warming
Beauty lies all around me
The blue sky with its scattered clouds
The hills with their winter greys and browns
Two cardinals fluttering from tree to tree
The sun shines ever so brightly
Providing glorious shadows and warmth
The stillness touches my heart
The beauty makes me smile
How glorious and blessed I am
Sharing a new day with my creator
Being a part of this daily ritual
My heart is truly singing
This morning I am blessed and grateful

OUR GIFT

Life is a gift
Not asked for but given
We can't choose our family,
How we look, or our talents
We absorb our environment,
Learn how to navigate within it
Some are born with challenges
Others seem to glide along life's path
We sometimes question why we are who we are
Why am I not as smart or as pretty as others?
Why am I not talented in music or art?
Why is my family not rich?
Why am I a minority treated of lesser worth?
Why was I born in a poor country?
Why do I have an illness or physical deformity?
There are so many "whys"
The gift of life includes the challenge
of building with the given

It includes embracing our environment
and making it better
Many gifts are needed to make the world better
Building a family or a community requires many talents
Struggles, disappointment, failures
are all part of our journey
Learning to overcome them is work
Those who destroy or devalue life
Waste a very valuable gift

WORDS

Words are powerful
Spoken every day, everywhere
They give meaning and purpose to life
Words inspire us to go beyond ourselves
To reach higher than we ever imagined

Words enable expression
How we use words affects our well being
Negative words create negative effects
Positive words lift our spirits

Words do matter
They inspire mankind to reach for the sky
They inform or diminish one's spirit
They determine who we become as a person
We are shaped by the words we think and express

LOVE IS ... ...

The feeling you never want to be apart
That special excitement you feel when you are together
Knowing that person is as important
to you as the air you breathe
Not imagining the future without the other in your life
A willingness to do the hard work of
positively sharing your life
Your ability to blend your dreams and support each other
Separating the problems from the love you share
Getting through the difficult times
with respect and kindness
Together adapting to the challenge's life brings
Respecting each other's individuality
Walking together, hand in hand to face the unknown
Beautiful, messy, challenging, difficult and amazing
A precious God-given gift
To be honored, cherished, and given
freely and without conditions

ESSENCE OF LOVE

Where there is love
The air feels lighter and purer
The heart beats a little faster
Life moves at a slower pace
Music often plays in your head
The wind gently blows through the trees
Love nurtures one's soul and spirit
Love connects us to another person
Blending and bonding together
Love can move slowly or fast
Sometimes instant and unsettling
Love is the anchor of life
Keeping one steadfast and whole
Giving purpose and direction
Love pushes one to evolve and grow
Often beyond our imagination and dreams
Love sustains us through difficulty and loss
Love is the foundation of life
What an amazing gift

CURIOSITY

Those who want to know ask why
How things work is a puzzle to be solved
It is like an ever-present itch
One that won't go away
The desire to know why or how is always there
It keeps toying at your mind and soul
It pushes you to ask questions
Galileo looked to the heavens and pondered the galaxies
He developed a telescope to see more
The Wright brothers imagined mankind flying
They developed a flying machine that created an industry
Marie Curie detected faint electrical currents in the air
An array of X-ray equipment has evolved
President Kennedy said America will go to the moon
Armstrong and Aldrin walked on the moon
Mankind's curiosity for knowledge is boundless
It is the engine that propels us forward
It is a gift that keeps on giving

(Dedicated to Dr. Patricia Meyers who grew tired
of me asking "why" in Neuroanatomy class. She
once told me "because a smart man said so".)

A TEXAS LEGEND'S LONG ROAD HOME

Our journey back to our family homeland was amazing and emotional. As little children, we heard our great Uncle Ed talk about the "old country". We didn't ask questions, but the memories stuck in our heads. The family was proud to be American, but memories of what became Germany were still vivid. They talked about the manor house and the land they deeded to Kaiser Wilhelm. There had been too many wars and they were leery of the changes that were coming.

America was a land of opportunities --a place to begin again. We never knew our great-grandfather and great-grandmother but appreciate and respect the sacrifices they made. Because they were willing to begin again, to dream big dreams and were hard workers, they gave us the gift of being Americans. We have been able to take advantage of opportunities presented. We hope we have given back to our country and have been a positive force for good.

There has always been a yearning to know more about the old country, to know about those who came before us. With the internet and its research and translation capabilities, we have traced our lineage back to the year 782. We know where the family name was first used, their bravery and perseverance, and that they were granted nobility around 800.

We know that around 1146 they moved up the Weser River to an area called Bad Essen and that they were granted land by Prince Philip Osnabruck. They built the first castle in the area and it was named Schloss Hunnefeld. As little children, we were told the family had a castle, but that it had gone out of the family. We never asked why. They left many letters, papers, documents, and family bibles that have served as a road map in developing our family history.

Family stories are important. They give one a sense of who they are. They serve as a guidepost and a way to see and feel continuity with the past. Ours guided us back to the "old country" and a chance to see and walk on land that belonged to our family for many centuries. We walked on steps that were part of the original castle that long ago was replaced.

It is awesome to walk where your ancestors lived and worked. I felt a part of them and that they stood with me.

SCHLOSS HUNNEFELD

The air was crisp and cool
The sun took turns peeking through the clouds
Schloss Hunnefeld majestically stood before us
The castle welcomed this day as she has for centuries
The first castle was long ago torn down
Remaining are rock steps, stone walls
and a tower along the canal
This land was granted to my ancestors in 1011
The original castle was the first castle built in the area

The current Castle has stood since the 1600's
She has withstood wars and difficult times
The spirit of this place remains strong
The von dem Busche family has loved and
cared for this special place since 1447
They continued the dreams of the von Hunnefelds
They have built upon their own dreams as well

The gardens had awakened for spring
The flowers and trees were in bloom
Ponds and bridges beckoned
The sunlight enhanced their color
There was a kind of magic that embraced this place

A feeling of peace, comfort and ancient beauty
A feeling of continuity with the past
Yet a feeling of life and presence all around

The pigeon tower stood tall and beautiful
A respite for these birds
All around were buildings and walls
Protectors in the past
Yet beauty to behold
I closed my eyes and imagined those who came before
I imagined their lives and their love of this land
I felt as if all the generations of von
Hunnefelds stood with me
I felt the spirit of their visions
Their dreams and hopes
I was blessed to walk where they walked
To see their dreams made real
Some left this dream and went to America
There they dreamed new dreams
There they began again
The old country always remained in their heart

GROWING OLD

When did it happen?
Where did the years go?
It seems like yesterday I was young
We were climbing trees
Swinging from the monkey bars in the back yard
Playing in the sand at the farm
Curled up reading Nancy Drew
Visiting cousins, playing in their canals
Life was simple but loads of fun

There were the high school years
Where lifelong friendships were made
So many have left us now
The memories seem like a blur
It came and went so fast

Becoming a new bride
Building a shared life
Learning to compromise and forgive
Sharing so many joys and sad times
Building a business together
Struggling to overcome heartaches and losses

Our greatest joys were the births of our daughters
Together we all learned this parenting thing
Bonding was instantaneous
Learning to become a family was amazing
Becoming a parent is the greatest gift one can receive.
It can be difficult, messy, challenging but so rewarding

Before you know it, there are grandchildren
Your children are parents
You look in the mirror and say it can't be
Somehow it doesn't fit the image you have of yourself
Somehow, the years slipped by when you were so busy
I look in the mirror and the years show
I thank God for the ride of my life.

ANOTHER TIME, ANOTHER PLACE

I close my eyes and remember
It doesn't seem so long ago
I begged for a poodle skirt
A crinoline petticoat and ballerina shoes
These were foreign to mother
She came of age during the great depression
Only necessities were on the needed list

Food was simple but delicious
Homemade cinnamon rolls to die for
Fresh vegetables, fruits and Jell-O salad of all kinds
Peanut butter sandwiches with
homemade jelly or sliced banana
Meals were a time for catching up
Everyone sat around the table

Church was an important influence on our lives
Sunday morning and evening services
Wednesday night activities
Summers at Alto Frio Baptist camp
Youth leaders whose influence remain with me
today. Unselfishly they gave of their time
Blessing the lives of those they touched

Big Band music and their singing stars
I love the music to this day
Their swing music touched our hearts
Our feet had to dance to songs like

Glen Millers "In the Mood" and "Moonlight Serenade"
Frank Sinatra's "Moon River" and "After the Loving"
Elvis Presley made the whole body move.
Pete Seeger, Woody Guthrie, Burl Ives and
others brought back folk music.

We loved hanging out at the local drive-in
It was the go-to place on dates
Dates were simple yet fun
Drive in movies, football games, eating watermelon,
drinking root beer floats, hanging out with friends, riding
the rides at Playland Park or miniature golf at Crestview
My heart sings when I remember these times

TO DREAM AGAIN

Has life taken its toll?
Have you locked away your dreams?
Find that discarded key that locked away those dreams
Unlock them and let them see light
Dreams are a gift to ourselves
An important part of who we are that needs light

Dreams give direction to our lives
Provide us with motivation and desire
Help us in decision making
Provide a roadmap for change and tomorrow

Open yourself up for new possibilities
Let your dreams form a basis for life's direction
Dreams can become reality
Move in the direction of new beginnings

GOLDEN GIRL

Four pounds of cuteness, bossiness and prissiness
Golden in color; strong in spirit
Her love is boundless
I picked her up and loved her instantly
She never shook or cried out
Our bond was immediate
I held her for hours
Her new home was embraced
She quickly ruled her new territory
A special furry gift when needed
She often stands her ground
But provides endless love
A constant source of joy, happiness and laughter
She helped me cope with loss of another love
She fills my day with love, laughter, and joy
A much loved and needed presence in my life

For Lolita, a very special golden Yorkie

BEAUTY IN THE LITTLE THINGS

We stand in amazement
Watching magnificent sunsets
We are inspired by mountains
And their sky-blue lakes
Multicolored sunsets that sweep across the sky
Take our breath away
The stars adorning the universe
Are breath taking in their majesty
But … … … … … …
Have you ever really looked at the little things?
A beautifully colored mammoth butterfly
Fluttering from flower to flower
A baby bird learning how to fly
Spreading its wings leaving the nest
A newborn baby fawn stumbling
As it tries to stand
Hummingbirds enjoying milkweed
A baby rabbit hopping behind its mother
Learning about its new world
A newborn puppy opening its eyes
Eager to explore its brave new world
Ready to steal someone's heart

SPRING DRIVE

Miles of yellow flowered fields
Bluebonnet clusters here and there
Bluffs revealing the winding Colorado River
Hills awash in varying shades of green and color
Wildflowers blooming along the roadway
Fields of spring bouquets awaiting a painter's canvass

History is all around
An early rock cottage stands in a cluster of trees
The roof has long ago deteriorated
A partial fireplace once provided warmth
Perhaps cooked meals on its coals
A welcoming porch is no longer there

The early Texas settlers experienced meager lives
Food had to be grown or killed
Isolation and loneliness were ever present
Yet they persevered and dreamed of a better tomorrow
Worked hard and built communities
As we travel the hills and valleys in the springtime
We give thanks for their contributions and big dreams
We marvel at the beauty all around

A one room schoolhouse sits alone
Resting under an arbor of trees
Students no longer seek knowledge within her walls
One wonders how many children
learned to read and write there
Studied mathematics, dreamed of a better tomorrow
Vowed to do their part in building
a welcoming community
Their spirit lives on as we meander along these backroads
Marveling at the beauty all around
Giving thanks for those who came before
They put down roots and began to build
They built a home, a community and a state

An old Rock Church signifies their
need for worshiping God
The old cemetery next to the church
was their final resting place
It is here that they had big dreams
and asked for God's help
I am grateful for their big dreams and their visions
I appreciate their dedication to doing the hard work
I hope I have added to their story.

THE GREY FOX

THE GREY FOX

There he sat
A perfect specimen
Perched on the rock ledge
He checks me out
Sitting perfectly still
Can he trust me?
Should he run?
He was grey with red streaks
I stand without movement
Admiring natures beauty
Trust can be difficult
Sometimes it can be life or death
Humans can be unpredictable
He decides I can be trusted
Slowly and quietly
He walks across the yard
Into the side yard
And out of view

(This beautiful specimen of nature lives in
the neighborhood but is rarely seen)

THE PERSIMMON TREE

She has stood for many years
Branches twisted and unique
People comment on how unusual she looks
She doesn't conform to the usual small tree
A Texas windstorm came roaring over the hills
It twisted and broke several main limbs
Now people say "cut it down"
"It is an old tree anyway"
My heart tells me NO!
It is ok to be different
The remaining branches give it a new shape
There is still life in the old tree
She will bloom again
The birds will enjoy the fruit
The shape will still be unique
Nonconformity can be a good thing
We have much to ponder
Being different can be inspiring

THE WORLD IS CHANGING

THE WORLD IS CHANGING

It came as an awakening
Maybe I don't belong anymore
The world has changed so much
It happened as I was busy
Suddenly I remembered mother
She told me the world was frightening
She worried about her grandchildren
For her, the world had become unfamiliar
Different from her own experiences
Recently, I experienced such thoughts

Mother stressed being a proper lady
Dressing appropriately for the occasion
Never forget your manners
Always respect your elders
Stay true to your beliefs
All these many years later
I still remember her teachings

I am grateful for her wisdom
It has served me well
Today her teachings are no longer the norm
My generation recovered from World War II
Only to fight in many more wars
We put men on the moon
Developed technology beyond our dreams
Somehow in the process of change
Older people were left behind

Computer technology and the World Wide Web evolved
Changing how we communicate
The world would never be the same
Artificial intelligence opened a world of opportunities
Going to Mars is now a reality, not a dream
It will bring unimaginable development and change
There appear to be no dreams that can't come true
That is the magic of our world

A REGRET

In the middle of millions
Sit the lonely
We pass them by daily
We live near them
They are sometimes our neighbors
Life is hectic
So much to do
Our schedules are full
Often focused on our tasks
We are truly unaware
Society has become self-centered
There are millions who live alone
Old age and illness are limiting
Often, they are victims of loneliness
They die in isolation
My heart is sad when I read their stories
I am reminded of elderly people
I waved to but never asked
"Can I do anything for you?"
I never took the time to chat
I never sought the wisdom that was theirs
I surely would have been blessed

THE WHITE SCARF

It was a long and brutal journey
Across North Africa they fought
Morocco, Tunisia, Algeria, Egypt
Across the Mediterranean to Sicily
Over to the boot of Italy and into the mountains
It was a hard fight day after day
Many soldiers lost their lives
The enemy was entrenched in the mountains
Machine guns rained down on them
Somehow, American soldiers got into the mountains
Battle after battle they fought their way up Italy
Changing the dynamics of WWII
Over the Alps they went into France
Many battles were fought in Eastern France
Germany was losing but still fighting
In a little village in Alsace Lorraine
As American soldiers were marching toward Germany
A woman ran up to my Uncle Wilmer
She handed him a hand-woven white scarf
"Soldier put this around your neck.
It will keep you warm."

An act of kindness in a battle-weary French village
The white scarf has been lost to time
All these many years later, I remember this story
I want this story to be remembered
This small act of kindness in a war-torn
French village should be remembered
This young American soldier came
home to Texas and built a life
He never forgot this French woman, her
kindness and the white scarf

(My Uncle Wilmer Howard fought under General George
S. Patton in the Mediterranean theater and in France)

LIFT OFF

The sky was a pale blue
Clouds were scattered across the horizon
It was a beautiful April day
Kennedy Space Center reverberated excitement
People seemed to be everywhere
On top of cars and rooftops
Up in the trees
Hanging out of upper windows
Standing on top of overpasses
Our small bus navigated through it all

My excitement was difficult to contain
The Center was full of anticipation
Excitement filled the air
My first view of STS-83 was astonishing
There she stood across the lake
A breathtaking view
The work of many thousands over years
Brought us to this incredible day
My heart was racing with excitement

We stood near the large clock
Watching the time go down
Only the lake stood between us and the Shuttle
Except for the alligators in the lake

As the clock showed one minute
Complete silence embraced us
At 30 seconds my heart and breath halted
Promptly on zero, the smoke began to billow upward
Completely embracing this magnificent structure
Slowly it began to rise toward the heavens
Disappearing over the horizon

This beautiful masterpiece of science and technology
Launched perfectly and as planned
STS-83 carried not only astronauts
It carried the hopes and dreams of many
It carried questions to be answered
It carried man's quest to understand the unknown

(April 4, 1997- A fuel cell problem
brought it home after 4 days.
Microgravity Science Laboratory- relaunched
on July 1, 1997 as STS-94)

NOTRE DAME

Notre Dame will rise again
Her towers and spheres will once again reach the sky
For over eight hundred years she has stood
A symbol of heritage, belief and beauty
Her frescos and sculptures will forever be remembered
Priceless paintings that were saved will again be enjoyed
The sounds of her organ reverberate in the heavens
She was built to provide awe and wonder
To provide the beauty of a belief in God.
She has stood since 1163
Built on the Ile de la Cite
The centuries of wear add to her charm
She has withstood revolutions, wars and time
She was memorialized by Victor Hugo
My heart aches today as I watch the
flames engulf her beauty
She will rise again and will again inspire those to come
I am honored to have experienced
her beauty and magnificence

4-15-2019
Placed poem on Facebook in tribute

WHY GOD WHY

I sit staring into space
Asking the eternal question
"Why God Why"
Mankind has pondered this question forever
Quarantine forces one to seek answers
Sometimes the answers just don't come
Forces around us confuse and distort one's thoughts
Strife, violence, name calling, and hate rule the day
The strength of our beliefs is challenged
Life, relationships, dreams and plans have changed
The foreseeable future seems bleak
How shall we adapt our lives?
What do we do with our dreams?
Shall we acquire new dreams?
There is one prevailing truth
Our lives have changed forever
We must navigate the changes.
Perhaps the path will become clear
We await the future.

MORNING LIGHT

Beaming through the half-closed shutter
Shine the early morning rays of light
Twinkling, lighting and welcoming a new day
New opportunities, new beginnings and new challenges
Each day's special gift with endless possibilities
The possibility of bringing joy to someone else
The possibility of learning a new skill
The possibility of creating something beautiful
The possibility of learning how to just be
The possibility of thanking those
who have blessed our life

WHEN GOD RODE SHOTGUN

It was a typical Texas summer day
Rain showers and lightning in the night
Sunshine with puffy clouds held the sky
The morning was perfect
It seemed like a good day to drive
The Texas Hill Country was beckoning
Home was two hours away
I headed up Hwy 281 in light traffic
The hills were varying shades of green
The creeks and rivers were full
Puffy clouds followed me north
The bottoms of the clouds were dark blue
Light summer showers blessed me for a few miles
An hour from home the clouds were bright
Rain had fallen earlier
The drive from 281 home is narrow
It gradually rises higher and higher
The hills cradle the Colorado River
Purposefully it enters Lake Travis
The area is beautiful and inspiring
I was slowly rising up a hill
Suddenly I am spinning
The car hit a large cedar tree

It was a hard hit
I kept spinning, hitting a second cedar tree
Finally, I hit a third cedar tree where the car lodged
I was eight feet down the hill
It was a long way to the bottom of the hill
I did not want the car to slide further
The airbag and the seatbelt had done their job
Carefully, I opened the door
I got myself out of the car
Other drivers had stopped
A man helped me up the hill to the road
A Travis County EMT nurse stopped
and called for assistance
My door was the only door that could open
Damage to my Prius was extensive
I know God was riding shotgun
My seat was the only part that was not crushed in
I said goodbye to my Prius
I thanked God for more time

(It was determined that I hit an oil and
water spot and hydroplaned)

OUTER BANKS AT EVENTIDE

The sand is slightly warm
The waves are moving inward
Washing my feet with the warm water
The sandcastles are awaiting the water
A seagull flies along the shore
Darting here and there
Awaiting the nightfall and rest
How peaceful the world seems
The western sky is ablaze
Manifesting the beauty of our world
All seems at peace
This moment along the sandy beach
Makes my heart sing
I breathe deeply
I listen to the cadence of the waves
I feel the movement of the water
Perhaps it will deposit shells in the sand
Driftwood polished by the water's movement
Maybe a long-lost treasure
Possibly a message in a bottle
The seagulls are preparing for nightfall
This moment in the sand at eventide blesses my soul

OUR SHINING STAR

Look to the eastern sky
There is a shining new star
The artistic, twinkling one
That's our beloved Becky
She greets us in the morning light
Reminding us that her spirit is with us
Says goodnight twinkling with mischievousness
Her beauty and artistic skill enhance the sky
Giving us a feeling of oneness of spirit
She enhanced the lives of all who knew her
We take comfort in all those memories
Feel blessed for the time we shared
Her beautiful soul, artistic skills and love strengthen us
We look to the heavens and feel her love
When we say goodnight
We look forward to the morning light
It reminds us of all the shared joy
Becky's beautiful spirit sustains us

A tribute to Rebecca (Becky) Breazeale Risor

NOTE

A little more than twenty years of my life were spent working on behalf of battered women and children. In retrospect, all my previous work experiences prepared me for this opportunity. While battering was part of my growing up experience, it was unspoken. I am eternally grateful for those years I met and worked for so many women and children who needed a helping hand and a safe place to make some difficult decisions. Laws that provided protection for battered women and their children were needed and quite challenging.

Working together with battered women, lawyers, Judges and legislatures, needed changes were made. Battering is still a problem but there are now resources and laws to better assist battered women and their children in getting out of an abusive relationship. It is a very complex problem. I salute those brave women who made some difficult decisions. The following two poems were written as a tribute to their strength and courage. No one should have to live in fear and abuse. We must stop accepting abusive behavior in families. It is not a personal matter. It is a human issue not to be tolerated,

THEY JUST KEEP COMING

They just keep coming
One after the other
Some come alone
Some bring children
Often with a few belongings
Usually in a black trash bag

Black and blue they come
Shattered, frightened, confused
Asking for safety and rest
Needing a respite from the violence
A place to gather thoughts
A place to process events

She says she loves him
She just wants him to love her
Doesn't understand why he beats her
Takes responsibility for his violence
Over and over, she asks herself
What did I do to make him so mad?

She seeks shelter to gather her thoughts
Her children are frightened and fearful
Life has become a continuous battle
Fear has become the norm
Obstacles are ever present
What options does she have?
The voices of battered women cry out

The world hears their voices
Do we still say it is a family matter?
Are we afraid to get involved?
Do we believe the woman asks for the abuse?
We must rise up and say NO MORE!!!

HEAR ME

He says he loves me
Yet he controls my total being
It is for my own good
My family causes problems; interferes
I need to stop my visits
My friends are not right for me
They are no longer welcome
Slowly my world is smaller and smaller

He calls throughout the day
Says he misses me
Asks where I am
I am punished for not being home
My world is shrinking
He threatens to teach me a lesson
My purpose is to serve him
Family and friends are distractions

When I have spoken up, he becomes enraged
I am thrown against the wall
Lifted slightly to make breathing difficult
His hand is on my mouth
My pet has been hurt during his rages
He tells the children to go to their rooms
Where they cling in fear
He threatens to hurt them

My world has shrunk
I live in constant fear
I can't please him
I pray for relief; for him to stop
I feel afraid and inadequate
Life has become a burden
All this in the name of love

UNCERTAINTY

Fear moves in and wraps itself around you
It tugs at the essence of your very being
Plants seeds of anxiousness and confusion
Cultivates uneasiness and is unsettling
Before one is aware, life is consumed
Fear, anxiety, confusion, the unknown rule
The winds of fear and darkness blow strong
One must call upon the Master Gardener
He has promised to hold us in his hand
To guide us through the unknown
To be a light through uncertainty
This is the time to look for the rainbows
Feel the blowing wind with pleasure
Enjoy the beauty that surrounds us
Let your spirit grow and bloom
There will be a beautiful tomorrow

THE ROAD OF LIFE

Sometimes the road of life is rocky and confusing
The terrain is difficult to navigate
Rocks and bumps; turns and hills
Navigating is difficult and confusing
We often ask ourselves Why?
How did I get on this course?
Can I find a smoother path?
These are the forever questions
Sometimes the path is accidental
Sometimes deliberately chosen
You must look deep inside
The answer may surprise you
Each of us in our own time
Seek the answer to these questions
The winding rocky roads
The hills and mountains
The valleys and rivers
The sometime confusing round abouts
The dead ends that sometimes stress us
The high freeways that seem to touch the sky
Each lead us along life's road
We must select our own path
To find the life we were meant to have

Proverbs 4:18
But the path of the righteous is like the light of dawn
that shines brighter and brighter until the full day.

FINDING HOPE

The tears occasionally flow
Sometimes unexpectantly and suddenly
Life seems on perpetual hold
Although life continues flowing forward
Dreams and life plans seem unreachable
Day after day; month after month
Safety and caution rule the day
We can't say goodbye to those we love
We hope they knew they were loved
Expendables ponder their worth
Struggle for a place in today's world
Fearful the virus will soon find them
Ending the few dreams and hopes left
Time is a gift when one is old
Each day is a special blessing
We must hang on to hope

ON BEING AFRAID

Sometimes life catches up with us
Sadness fills our heart and soul
We keep smiling, sometimes laughing
Yet pain and fear lurk inside
Life can be unsettling and frightening
Sometimes full of pain and despair
So much sadness and hopelessness all around
Tragedy daily unfolds across the world
Our hearts feel as if they will break
It is difficult to absorb all the pain, death and violence
Anxiety and fear creep into our thoughts
It would seem that all is lost
It is these times when I remember
"Be still and know that I am God"
"All things work together for good
for those that love the Lord"
"I can do all things through Him who strengthens me"

Psalms 46:10
Romans 8:28
Philippians 4:13

FRIENDS

One by one
Each in their own time
They have left us
So many years have passed
Our school years are distant memories
Our lives took us to different places
Each made their mark in their own way
Contributing positively
Making the world better
Time has said to some
It is time to rest
Your job is done
One day I will join them
Today I am remembering
Their kindnesses and specialness
How wonderful friendship has been
So much joy, strength and support
Each friendship has brought to me
I miss you very much
I will always hold you in my heart
In that special friendship place

CHOICES

The morning sun is peeking over the horizon
Grateful for another day
I can choose how I will use this day.
Shall I join the hustle and bustle of the daily tasks?
Perhaps take a walk and explore nature?
Call a friend and catch up?
Take a ride in the countryside?
Explore small nearby towns for treasures of the past?
Sit and observe the sun sparkles on the lake?
Life gives us possibilities and choices
How we use them is up to us
Have a great day

EXIT

When it comes my time to exit
Know how blessed I was
Life has given me much
Challenges and blessings
Friendships and love
Gratefulness and wonder
Opportunity and loss
Each woven into my unique design
Woven on the loom of life
My hope and prayer remain
Perhaps I made a small difference

04164560-00961966

Printed in the United States
by Baker & Taylor Publisher Services